Original title:
Narrow Paths Under the Witch Damp

Author: Aron Pilviste
ISBN HARDBACK: 978-1-80563-022-7
ISBN PAPERBACK: 978-1-80564-543-6

Midnight Wanderings through Faceless Trails

Beneath the silver, shimmering moon,
I stroll through whispers in the night,
Where shadows leap, and secrets croon,
The world awakes to hidden light.

Branches sway with tales of old,
Each step I take feels gently bold,
A rustle here, a fleeting breath,
In solitude, I dance with death.

The forest hums a lullaby,
As stars align in cosmic grace,
I lose myself, let moments fly,
And wander in this timeless space.

A fox appears, its eyes aglow,
Guiding me where wonders weave,
Through faceless trails where wild things grow,
In every turn, a chance to believe.

With each heartbeat, the night expands,
A magic swirling all around,
In midnight's grasp, I join the bands,
Of dreams awakened from the ground.

The Crush of Leaves Underfoot

The autumn's breath, crisp and bold,
Whispers stories yet untold,
Each leaf that falls, like gilded dreams,
A symphony of rustling schemes.

They crunch beneath my wandering feet,
A melody, both soft and sweet,
In every step, a pact, a pact,
With earth and sky, a gentle act.

Golden hues and fiery red,
Nature's quilt, a pathway spread,
Through forests deep, I find my way,
As leaves cascade and dance, they sway.

Each breath I take, the silence breaks,
With echoes of the past it makes,
The crush of leaves, a song reborn,
In fleeting moments, hearts are torn.

I pause to soak this beauty in,
As twilight drapes the world in sin,
Each step a prayer, each path a friend,
Through autumn's grace, we find our end.

Cascading Shadows of Enchantment

In twilight's veil, the shadows bloom,
They stretch and bend, a soft perfume,
With whispers spun in threads of light,
A dance unfolds, a magic flight.

The trees stand tall, in silent cheer,
Their leaves a tapestry of year,
As nighttime slowly wraps the scene,
Cascading dreams in shades of green.

Each flicker sparks a tale untold,
Of wizards, creeks, and hearts of gold,
In every flutter, a mystery weaves,
Where enchantments whisper through the leaves.

The moon hangs low, a lantern bright,
Illuminating hidden sights,
In shadows deep, we chase the trace,
Of spirits lost, in time and space.

With every step, the night reveals,
A world that spins on softest wheels,
Cascading shadows, secrets cast,
In this enchanted realm, we're vast.

Bewildering Turns of the Graying Path

Upon the edge of twilight's grasp,
I wander through the misty past,
The path ahead, a winding lore,
With turns that lead to distant shores.

Each step I take, the unknown calls,
A siren's song through forest walls,
With shadows lengthening in my wake,
I find the choices I must make.

The trees, they whisper words of fate,
As leaves begin to twist and grate,
In glimmers lost, a memory swells,
Through graying paths where wonder dwells.

I pause and breathe the musty air,
A moment's doubt, a fleeting stare,
Then forge ahead, with heart held fast,
Embracing all that will come last.

With every turn, new sights reveal,
The wondrous truths that time can heal,
Bewildering paths, yet I persist,
In this grand dance, I must exist.

Whispers in the Thicket

In the quiet thicket, secrets weave,
Tales of magic, none believe.
Beneath the boughs, where shadows stir,
Whispers hum, soft as a blur.

A flicker of light, a glimmer of hope,
The path unfolds, like a slippery slope.
Echoes of laughter, lost in the haze,
Dance with the leaves in a curious craze.

Footsteps echo on soft, mossy ground,
Mysterious creatures dart all around.
With every heartbeat, the forest sighs,
A world alive beneath ancient skies.

In tangled vines, a story untold,
Adventures await, both daring and bold.
The thicket beckons, enchantments await,
Where magic lives, and dreams oscillate.

So tread with caution, O wanderer brave,
For secrets lie hidden, the thicket will save.
In the depths of the wild, the truth softly calls,
Whispers of destiny echoing through walls.

Shadows of the Enchanted Trail

Through shadows that dance, the trail unwinds,
In the heart of the woods, where silence binds.
Golden leaves flutter, kissed by the air,
A path of enchantment, laid with great care.

Beneath the twilight, where dreams intertwine,
The magic of twilight begins to align.
Each step reveals a glimmering light,
That guides weary souls through the velvet night.

A rustle of wings, as night creatures soar,
The distant call of the mystical lore.
Every twist, every turn, holds stories untold,
Of brave hearts and legends, both daring and bold.

The shadows grow long, but hope lingers near,
In the hush of the forest, whispers appear.
With stars overhead, like diamonds that play,
The enchanted trail unfolds a new day.

Secrets Beneath the Canopy

Beneath the canopy, where shadows reside,
Lies an ancient world, where secrets abide.
The trees keep their stories, from years long gone,
In the rustling leaves, a forgotten song.

Dappled sunlight filters, through branches so wide,
Unveiling the secrets that nature can hide.
A harmony whispers, from roots deep below,
Echoing tales that the wild winds forego.

Creatures of wonder, in silence they tread,
Guardians of mysteries, their paths softly spread.
Each footfall conceals a saga of lore,
Of brave souls who wander, and cherished folklore.

Glimmers of magic in air thick with dreams,
In the heart of the forest, where nothing is as it seems.
The canopy sighs, with secrets to spin,
Inviting the curious, the brave, to begin.

Twilight's Forbidden Walk

In twilight's embrace, a journey is cast,
Where moonlight shimmers, shadows are vast.
With every soft whisper, the night starts to fade,
And hints of enchantment dance in the glade.

The path of the stars leads the way through the dark,
Where dreams take flight, igniting a spark.
Each step through the mist sings secrets, untold,
In twilight's arms, the brave hearts are bold.

Treading the line where both worlds meet,
The spirit of magic flows underfoot's beat.
With courage as armor, they scribe their own fate,
What lies in the shadows, they dare to create.

But with beauty comes caution, the sirens' sweet song,
For twilight's enchantment can lead one astray.
A delicate balance, a dance most divine,
In the twilight's forbidden walk, stories entwine.

Ghostly Whispers in the Wilderness

In shadows deep the phantoms sigh,
Through tangled roots where spirits lie.
An echo calls from time long past,
In twilight's grip, the die is cast.

The ancient trees with whispers weave,
Their stories told for those who grieve.
Each breeze a tale of lost delight,
In the stillness of the night.

A flicker glows where lanterns fade,
In hidden paths, their secrets laid.
With every step, the mist unfurls,
Beneath the moon, a world of pearls.

Through fog and foghorns, shadows creep,
Where quiet forms and silence seep.
Their haunting calls, a soft lament,
In nature's breath, our hearts are bent.

And as the darkness swells with dreams,
The past awakens, nothing seems.
In ghostly whispers, truth is spun,
In wilderness, we are but one.

Forbidden Glades and Enchanted Mists

In glades where few have ever trod,
The whispers stir the twilight odd.
With gossamer and moonlit threads,
The forest holds what heartache dreads.

Enchanted mists come soft and sly,
As shadows flicker, dreams comply.
In every rustle, tales take flight,
In faerie's grasp, erasing fright.

With crystal dew upon the leaves,
A realm that beggars gentle thieves.
Beware the charm that binds the bold,
In glades of wonder, things are sold.

A single wish, a fleeting glance,
Can lead a heart into a dance.
But tread with care, for magic's guise,
May cloud your judgment, seal your ties.

Yet still the call to wander stirs,
Where laughter mingles with the purrs.
In every clearing, a secret glows,
In forbidden glades, where magic flows.

The Cloaked Venture of the Night

In twilight's cloak, the shadows slide,
With every step, the night confides.
A venture born of whispered wishes,
In hidden paths, the dark augments.

The silver moon, a watchful eye,
Guides wanderers beneath the sky.
Through whispered fears and starlit dreams,
Forever bound by moonlit seams.

The cloak of night, both warm and cold,
Enfolds the tales that darkness told.
In secret corners and veils of mist,
Adventures lie, yet to be kissed.

Through brambles thick and shadows deep,
The heart can find its way to keep.
Each venture born from quiet sighs,
In cloaked embrace, the world defies.

And when the dawn begins its chase,
The night retreats, a fleeting space.
Yet in the heart where shadows lay,
The cloaked venture leads us away.

Beneath the Witches' Boughs

Beneath the boughs where shadows dance,
The witches weave their secret chance.
With herbs and salt, their potions swirl,
In crooked paths, the fates unfurl.

A cauldron bubbling, dreams arise,
In every spell, a truth belies.
Their laughter chirps like distant bells,
In midnight hours, where magic dwells.

And as the night wraps tight around,
The whispers of enchantment sound.
With every twig that breaks in fright,
The wild blooms blossom, spirits light.

Through thicket thick and foggy seams,
They chase the echoes of their dreams.
Invisible threads between us bind,
In witching hours, the heart untwined.

So heed the call beneath the leaves,
For what you seek, the night believes.
In twilight's clutch, all wonder grows,
Beneath the witches' boughs, love flows.

Treading Softly through the Unseen

In shadowed paths where whispers dwell,
The moonlight dances, casting spells.
With every footstep, silence grows,
Unseen spirits brush like gentle snow.

Through ancient trees, the secrets sway,
They call the wanderer to stay.
Each rustling leaf, a tale to share,
Of worlds unseen, of dreams laid bare.

The nightingale sings, a haunting tune,
Guiding the heart 'neath the silver moon.
With every breath, the magic flows,
In unseen realms where wonder glows.

Softly treading, heart in tune,
The stars above hum a gentle boon.
In twilight's grasp, the journey starts,
For those who wander, to find their hearts.

The Cursed Crossroads of Eld

In shadows thick, the crossroads lie,
Where choices wane and dreams do die.
The lantern flickers, hope may fade,
With every step, the past is weighed.

Whispers echo through the air,
Of souls entwined in deep despair.
With paths that twist like tangled vines,
The cursed fate of ancient signs.

Faceless shadows stretch and moan,
In dread of journeys left alone.
Yet courage breathes in lingering light,
To face the darkness, reclaim the night.

A raven caws from branches high,
Guiding hearts where fears may lie.
At each fork, a truth unveiled,
As through the night, the brave are hailed.

Haunting Blossoms in the Dusk

In twilight's glow, the blossoms bloom,
Their petals whisper of joy and gloom.
In fragrant wafts, the memories seep,
Of love lost deep, in silence keep.

Each flower bends with burdened grace,
Hiding secrets in their embrace.
Their colors bleed beneath the sky,
A tapestry of dreams gone by.

The wind carries echoes, soft and clear,
Of laughter shared, now tinged with fear.
Yet in the night, their spirits sing,
Of hope reborn in the new spring.

Beneath the stars, lost souls may find,
Haunting blossoms, love entwined.
In every petal, a story sways,
A dance of shadows beneath the rays.

Winding Through the Sorcery of Old

In ancient tomes where shadows weave,
Lies magic bound that souls believe.
With every word, the air alights,
A whispering spell in the still of nights.

Through hidden glades, the secrets flow,
In silvered streams where wildflowers grow.
Each step, a charm, each breath, a sigh,
As time unravels, the spirits fly.

With elixirs brewed from stardust dreams,
The heart awakens, the soul redeems.
In laughter soft and battles bold,
The stories bind through sorcery of old.

In twilight's glow, the candles burn,
For those who seek, the wheel will turn.
With every glance, the magic swells,
In winding paths where enchantment dwells.

At the Edge of the Sylvan Mystery

Whispers of shadows softly tread,
Where ancient trees weave tales long dead.
Moonlight dances on a silver stream,
Guiding lost souls to a waking dream.

In the glen where the nightingale sings,
Secrets of time twine with hidden wings.
A silver mist shrouds the silent glade,
Veiling the paths that the wise have made.

Flickers of magic brush past the night,
Glimmers of hope in the heart's delight.
A call from the depths of the darkened wood,
Where enchantment whispers, misunderstood.

Step lightly on moss where the faeries play,
Let the laughter of leaves fill the fray.
Each step a journey through tangled lore,
Where past and present entwine evermore.

The edge of the sylvan stands close yet far,
A portal awaits beneath every star.
With courage as guide, dare the unknown,
For within the forest, the truth is sown.

The Wanderer's Promise in the Gloom

Under the canopy thick with despair,
The wanderer's heart beats with hope rare.
Through fog and shadows, the path remains,
A promise, a beacon in twilight's chains.

Footsteps echo on the path of old,
Each mark a tale yet to be told.
With every breath, the night reveals,
The courage that time and darkness seals.

Stars flicker above like a distant dream,
Guiding the seeker on a restless stream.
In the clutch of night, solitude sways,
Yet the wanderer's spirit, forever stays.

In hidden corners where dreams align,
A vow of courage, steadfast, divine.
The whispering winds carry tales anew,
Of battles fought and promises true.

So walk, dear soul, with your heart in hand,
Through the gloom, where the lost understand.
Each step a promise, each breath a spark,
Illuminating wisdom in shadows' dark.

Enchanted Roots of the Forest Floor

Beneath the boughs where the wild things grow,
The roots entangle beneath, down low.
Whispers of ancient tales softly creep,
In the heart of the forest where secrets sleep.

Moss-covered stones guard the quiet old,
A tapestry woven from nature's bold.
Each leaf a story, each branch a sigh,
Beneath the expanse of the starlit sky.

In twilight's embrace, the earth comes alive,
With hidden wonders that strive and thrive.
The pulse of the woods echoing low,
In harmony with twilight's gentle flow.

Deep in the thicket, shadows take flight,
Dancing through the veil of encroaching night.
Beneath the roots where the magic swells,
Lies an enchanted realm where no one dwells.

So linger awhile where the wild things play,
Let the spirit of nature whisk you away.
For within every whisper, the earth will share,
The tales of the forest, alive, aware.

Dreams Twined in Lurking Vines

In the thicket where the shadows blend,
Lurking vines twist and elegantly bend.
Whispers float on the cool evening air,
A tapestry woven with delicate care.

Night blooms softly, perturbing the dark,
Dreams take flight on a fragile lark.
Each petal a key to the hidden heart,
Where secrets unfurl and mysteries start.

Through tangled trails, the unknown calls,
To wanderers bold who heed its thralls.
With every thorn, a lesson learned,
In the embrace of nature, life is earned.

Glimmers of wonder peek through the green,
Visions awaken where fears have been.
For in the wild's arms, the soul finds flight,
Carried away on the wings of night.

So tread with grace in this realm divine,
Where dreams are woven in lurking vine.
Each step a dance on the edge of fate,
An adventure awaits; do not hesitate.

The Lonesome Call of the Misty Woods

In the deep of night, where shadows creep,
Whispers arise from woods so deep.
Moonlight dances on leaves so fair,
Calling the dreamers from their lair.

Fog weaves tales in the silent air,
Secrets hidden, they softly share.
Ancient spirits roam with grace,
Their laughter echoes in this place.

Beneath the boughs, the heart beats slow,
Every step leads where few dare go.
Through tangled roots and brambles wide,
The lonesome call is a haunting guide.

A rustle stirs the midnight haze,
Leading lost souls to a secret maze.
Fireflies flicker in a dance so rare,
Guiding the wanderers unaware.

Morning light unveils the wood's embrace,
Soft whispers fade, yet still leave a trace.
With every dawn, magic starts anew,
The misty woods, forever true.

Lighthouses of the Sorcerer's Realm

Amidst the waves, where wild winds wail,
Stand sturdy towers, with tales to unveil.
Guardians bright, they guide the lost
In a world where shadows pay the cost.

Each lantern burns with a spell so old,
Casting warmth on hearts that are bold.
Glowing gems in a tempest's grip,
A beacon of hope on a treacherous trip.

Through storms and silence, their glow remains,
A symphony sung in the ocean's veins.
Wizards watch from their lofty heights,
Chasing the dark with shimmering lights.

Whispers of sailors, long gone from the sea,
Echo through halls, where spells wander free.
These lighthouses hold ancient dreams,
In the heart of nights bathed in moonbeams.

In twilight's glow, the magic ignites,
Casting long shadows in magical flights.
Here, worlds collide and destinies swell,
In the lighthouses of the sorcerer's spell.

Timeless Journeys through Sylvan Shadows

Through verdant paths where secrets lie,
The sylvan shadows beckon nigh.
Whispers linger on the breeze,
Calling forth wanderers with ease.

Each leaf a tale, each root a song,
In the forest's heart, where all belong.
Time is woven in every thread,
Stitched with dreams of the long since fled.

Glimmers peek through the emerald veil,
Guiding souls on a mystic trail.
Where echoes dance and spirits play,
In timeless journeys, night turns to day.

Ancient oaks stand wise and tall,
Guardians of legends that never fall.
Each step leads deeper into lore,
And opens wide the whispered door.

Moonbeams trickle like silver streams,
Weaving through shadows, igniting dreams.
With each heartbeat, the forest sighs,
As timeless secrets meet bright skies.

Ensnared by Echoes and Enchantment

In the twilight's grasp, where echoes dwell,
Enchantment lingers, weaving its spell.
Voices from ages long since gone,
Dance through the night, till the break of dawn.

Through glades of wonder, softly they call,
A shimmering tune that captivates all.
Lost in their magic, hearts intertwine,
With every note, the stars brightly shine.

Mirrors of twilight reflect the past,
Whipers of fate that are meant to last.
Softly they tug at the heart's embrace,
Guiding the lost to their rightful place.

Spirits of music, ageless and free,
Guardians of dreams, mere mortals can see.
Under their spell, tempests turn mild,
As echoes cradle the forgotten child.

A portrait of magic, alive in the night,
With every sigh, the world feels right.
Ensnared by echoes, by love's sweet chance,
Underneath starlight, we all find romance.

A Lament Amongst the Ancient Trees

Beneath the boughs where shadows weave,
The whispers of the past do grieve.
In twilight's hush, their tales unfold,
Of secrets lost and dreams of old.

The branches sway with gentle sighs,
As memories dance 'neath fading skies.
With every rustle, echoes call,
In the heart of woods, we feel it all.

Mossy stones hold faint regrets,
In nature's arms, our sorrow rests.
Yet beauty blooms where darkness lay,
Embracing night to greet the day.

The forest sings, a haunting tune,
Of love and loss beneath the moon.
Each leaf a token, every breeze,
A lullaby that stirs the trees.

So here I stand, in solemn grace,
Amidst the roots, I find my place.
In ancient woods, my heart will stay,
A lament soft as the twilight's sway.

Vows in the Charmed Wilderness

In the clearing where the wildflowers bloom,
Our promises rest beneath the moon.
With tender glances, our hearts align,
In the chase of magic, your hand in mine.

The twinkling stars, like watchers above,
Witness the vows we whisper of love.
In the twilight's glow, we'll weave our fate,
In a tapestry none can recreate.

With every breeze, a sweet refrain,
In the wilderness, joy will remain.
Through tangled paths and shadows cast,
We'll forge a bond that forever lasts.

The forest blooms with promises bright,
As we pledge our love in the soft moonlight.
With nature's grace as our guiding star,
Together, love shall carry us far.

In the heart of wild, where spirits sing,
We write our vows on the winds of Spring.
A sacred dance in the twilight's embrace,
In this enchanted, timeless place.

The Unending Glimmer of Hallowed Roads

Along the paths where memories tread,
The glimmering lights of tales long spread.
With each step taken, shadows greet,
In this hallowed place, where time's discreet.

The cobblestones hold laughter's trace,
Whispers of lovers in their embrace.
Each turn reveals a story untold,
In the glimmer of paths, our hopes unfold.

With every dawn, new journeys rise,
Beneath the watchful, open skies.
In the breath of wind and song of birds,
We find our truth in the magic of words.

The footfalls echo, a gentle rhyme,
As we wander through the folds of time.
Each fleeting moment a spark ignites,
In the tapestry of days and nights.

So let us roam where the heart beholds,
The unending tales that fate unfolds.
In the glimmering light of the winding ways,
We'll cherish the journey, come what may.

Ensnared by the Phantom Glade

In shadows deep, the whispers sigh,
A glade where moonlight dares not pry.
The trees like giants, silence grips,
And secrets dwell on cloaked lips.

With every step, the air grows thick,
A haunting tune, a spectral trick.
Lost in paths where time stands still,
Charmed by echoes, bent to will.

A shimmer glows, a glint of fate,
What stirs within this hidden gate?
The heartbeats quicken, fear takes hold,
In twilight's clutch, the brave turn cold.

Yet still there lingers, a glint of hope,
A thread of light that helps us cope.
Though shadows dance and phantoms reign,
The dawn will rise, through all the pain.

The Mournful Lament of That Which Lurks

Beneath the soil, the whispers crawl,
A presence felt, yet never seen at all.
Restless spirits in the night,
Forever bound, forsaking light.

They wail a tune, a sad refrain,
Of fleeting joy, of lingering pain.
In midnight hours, their sorrow flows,
A tale of love that darkness knows.

From hollowed depths, a shadow stirs,
A haunting echo that now blurs.
With every pause, a heartbeat lost,
In battles fought, in dreams embossed.

Yet in the gloom, a flicker burns,
Of fierce desires, that heart yearns.
And in that ache, a truth unspooled,
The love once lost, the brave, the fooled.

Spiraling Desires Through Gloomy Thorns

In tangled thorns, the dreams take flight,
A dance of wishes cloaked in night.
Each petal frail, each stem a scar,
Yet beauty blooms where shadows are.

The heart, it twists in shadows' grip,
Yearning always for a lover's kiss.
Yet tangled pathways, paved with doubt,
Can lead the soul too far about.

With every turn, the darkness sighs,
A bittersweet taste beneath the skies.
Desires spiraling, wild and free,
Through thorns that whisper, "Come to me."

But to embrace what lies ahead,
One must confront what's deeply fed.
Perhaps beyond the bramble's snare,
A truth awaits, stripped down and bare.

Embraced by Midnight's Trickery

When twilight falls, the shadows dance,
In jest and whim, they seize their chance.
With gleaming eyes and laughter light,
They weave enchantments in the night.

The moon, a witness to their games,
Reflecting light while hiding names.
In mischief's grasp, we lose our way,
Entranced by visions that softly sway.

Yet in the depths of blinding flair,
There's magic strong, a subtle dare.
To brave the dark, to seek the truth,
For wisdom often lies in youth.

So heed the whispers, trust the call,
For in the night, we rise or fall.
Embraced by trickery's soft grin,
We find the strength to start again.

Beneath the Shroud of the Desserted Vale

Beneath the shroud of ancient stone,
The whispers of the lost are grown.
In shadows deep, their secrets hide,
A tale of sorrow, long denied.

The winds that sigh through rustling leaves,
Speak tales of heartache, no one sees.
In twilight's grasp, where echoes dwell,
The vale keeps secrets, none can tell.

Forgotten paths where footsteps fade,
Harness the dreams of past parades.
With every stone, a heart once beat,
In silence linger, bittersweet.

The moonlight dances on gravel bare,
Casting shadows, a gentle care.
Each glimmer holds a memory tight,
A fleeting glimpse of lost delight.

So wander here, where time stands still,
And listen close, obey the thrill.
For in the vale, where whispers weave,
A world of magic we'll receive.

Murmurs of the Spirits in the Shade

In the shade where spirits dwell,
Murmurs weave a timeless spell.
Softly dancing through the night,
Faint reflections, pale as light.

Leaves are rustling, secrets shared,
Among the roots, the silence bared.
Each sigh holds a distant tear,
Echoes whispering when near.

In hidden glades where shadows rest,
Ghostly forms feel less than blessed.
With gentle hands, they brush the ground,
In softest whispers, souls unbound.

A flicker here, a shimmer there,
Tales of longing fill the air.
Their stories linger in the breeze,
Among the boughs of ancient trees.

As twilight fades into the dawn,
The spirits rise, but dreams move on.
Yet in the shade, where murmurs grow,
Their haunting tales forever flow.

The Echo of Forgotten Dreams

In a world where whispers linger,
The echoes of dreams, a ghostly singer.
Beneath the surface of the night,
They send their wishes taking flight.

Forgotten hopes on winds do ride,
In every corner where shadows hide.
With every pulse of fading light,
Dreams drift softly, out of sight.

Once bright and bold, now cloaked in mist,
The tender dreams that time has kissed.
In silent realms of deep despair,
Their stories dwell, elusive air.

But in the silence, whispers call,
For every rise, there comes a fall.
Yet echoes linger, strong and clear,
In every heart, they persevere.

So search for threads that time forgot,
In darkened corners, seek the spot.
The dreams once lost can find their way,
And bloom anew, come what may.

Lost Moments in the Veil of Maw

In the veil of maw where shadows blend,
Lost moments linger, never end.
Fleeting whispers of what was real,
In twilight's grasp, we twist and squeal.

Glimmers fade as the dusk descends,
Time meanders, it twists and bends.
Captured glances, a fleeting show,
In the depths where memories glow.

Voices calling from depths of night,
Each lost moment a flickering light.
In memories forged and time unspooled,
Between the breaths, our lives are ruled.

With every heartbeat, time does wane,
Yet in the dark, there lies no shame.
For all we've lost, we'll find again,
In shadows deep or soft refrain.

So dance with echoes, embrace the fall,
In the veil of maw, we'll hear the call.
For every moment lost is found,
In the heartbeat of this hallowed ground.

Entwined Footsteps Through Eldritch Briars

In shadows deep where whispers weave,
The tangled paths no heart could leave.
Eldritch briars grasp and moan,
With every step, their secrets grown.

Two souls walk where magic stirs,
Chasing dreams, their vision blurs.
Through thorny threads of time and mist,
Each heartbeat draws them, hand and fist.

In haunted glades where fates entwine,
The air hums soft, a spell divine.
Together bound, through night they sail,
With every challenge, they prevail.

The moon above a silver guide,
In murmurings, their fears subside.
Through tangled roots and bitter bramble,
The light of love, a flick'ring candle.

So tread they forth, this fated pair,
In worlds unseen, they've laid their care.
Entwined they dance through mystic lies,
With hope reflected in their eyes.

Where the Mists Embrace the Veiled

Where mists do curl and shadows glide,
The veils of night in secrets hide.
A world anew, with wonders tight,
In twilight's grasp, the dreams take flight.

With every step, the whispers bloom,
In silent halls, they chase the gloom.
The echoes soft, a haunting song,
In this embrace, they both belong.

Footfalls trace a path unknown,
Where stars awaken, softly shone.
The veil lifts gently, secrets bare,
In woven tales, they weave the air.

As dawn approaches, kisses mist,
The veiled truth winks, and fate's a twist.
A journey marked by fate and chance,
Where spirits waltz in phantom dance.

So let them roam through fog and light,
In dreams entwined, they lose their fright.
A realm where mists and shadows meet,
In whispered vows, their love's complete.

Crossroads of Starlit Sorrows

Beneath the arch of sky's embrace,
Lie crossroads marked by love, and grace.
Each star a tear, each tear a plea,
In silent night, their spirits flee.

With open hearts, they meet despair,
Yet find the light in darkest air.
For every sorrow, starlit bright,
A beacon burns, igniting night.

They gather near, where shadows tread,
With quiet hope and words unsaid.
At every turn, new paths unfold,
In gentle whispers, tales retold.

Bound by the weight of destinies,
Their hands entwined, like roots of trees.
The silent strength in shared goodbyes,
Invisible threads, with love that ties.

In this vast web of fate's design,
They shine like stars, their hearts align.
Across the void, their voices soar,
At crossroads where starlit sorrows pour.

Treading Lightly Through the Gloom

In tangled woods where shadows creep,
They tread with care, their hearts to keep.
Each step a prayer, each breath a plea,
For light amidst the dark sea.

Through branches low and thorns that bite,
They search for warmth, a spark of light.
With whispered words that dance and weave,
In every moment, they believe.

Gloom wraps tight like a velvet cloak,
Yet in its grasp, new bonds evoke.
In quiet strength, beneath the weight,
They forge a path; they twist their fate.

Together strong, through thick and thin,
In whispered songs, their joys begin.
With hope that flutters like a dove,
They weave their way through gloom with love.

And when the dawn breaks soft and true,
They find a world awash in dew.
Through trials faced, their spirits bloom,
Forever free, beyond the gloom.

Lost Wanderings in Forbidden Glades

In twilight's cloak where shadows creep,
The lost ones wander, secrets deep.
Among the trees that softly sigh,
Their whispers float against the sky.

Footsteps echo on leaf-strewn ground,
Where ancient magic hums around.
The glades, they hold in silence tight,
The dreams of those who lost the light.

A flicker here, a shimmer there,
The dance of fates entwined with care.
Through every thicket, misty veil,
The heartbeats quicken, voices pale.

In shadows cast, the spirits play,
Entwined with night, they roam astray.
A call, a pull, their whispers tease,
In hidden glades, they find their ease.

Yet, as the dawn begins to break,
The paths once lost, now seem awake.
And those who quest through dusk and fright,
Shall find their way in morning light.

Beneath the Boughs of Eldritch Whispers

Beneath the boughs of timeless trees,
Where every rustle stirs the breeze,
The whispers weave through twilight's shroud,
A tale of magic, sweet and loud.

In shadows deep, the spirits wait,
To guide the brave, to tempt their fate.
Through gnarled roots and winding trails,
The heart beats strong as fear prevails.

With every step, the world may shift,
Unraveling the ancient rift.
A tapestry of time unfolds,
A story silenced, yet retold.

In hidden glades, the echoes sing,
Of battles fought and loves in spring.
The woodland sings its haunting tune,
Beneath the watchful, silver moon.

Oh, wanderers lost, heed the call,
For in the whispers, find your all.
The dance of fate, the pull of true,
Beneath the boughs, a world anew.

The Charms of Forgotten Paths

The paths once bright have faded dim,
Yet still they sing a lonesome hymn.
In ivy cloaks and twilight's breath,
They beckon softly, hint of death.

With every leaf that rustles slow,
A secret waits, a tale to show.
The charms of old, from time untold,
In every fork, a dream unfolds.

Among the ferns and tangled vines,
A shimmered light, where truth aligns.
With courage drawn from deep within,
The heart must leap, the soul must spin.

In echoes soft, the spirits nigh,
Remind us all of how to fly.
Through winding ways, the past will guide,
As memory whispers, there's no pride.

Oh, search the woods for what is lost,
Each step you take, remember cost.
The charms of paths beneath the jade,
Awake the dreams that once had played.

Secrets of the Woodland Spirits

In woodlands deep, where shadows dance,
The spirits whisper, lost in trance.
Their secrets flow through ancient trees,
In every rustle, every breeze.

With glimmers bright, they lead the way,
Through hidden glades where lost souls stray.
A flicker here, a fleeting sound,
In nature's heart, their truths abound.

They guard the tales of ages past,
In every whisper, spells are cast.
With gentle hands, they weave the night,
The moonlit paths, a guiding light.

As dawn awakes and shadows fade,
The secrets shared in hush are laid.
With open hearts, the brave explore,
Embrace the magic forevermore.

So wander forth, dear wanderer brave,
In nature's arms, your spirit save.
For woodland spirits, wise and true,
Shall guard the secrets held in you.

The Fading Light of Hidden Shadows

In the twilight where whispers dwell,
Shadows stretch, weaving their spell.
The echoes call, a gentle sigh,
As day concedes to the evening sky.

Flickering stars begin to bloom,
In corners dark, they chase the gloom.
Each glimmered light hides a tale,
Of spirits lost, and dreams that pale.

Through tangled woods, the secrets glide,
With time's embrace, they gently bide.
Yet in the dusk, a spark remains,
A hope that shines through ancient chains.

Beneath the boughs where shadows play,
Whispers of twilight softly sway.
The fading light, a canvas bare,
Brushes the night with silver hair.

So listen close, and you may find,
In hidden realms, the ties that bind.
A flickering hope among the seeds,
Of fading light and forgotten deeds.

Unseen Eyes in the Thickets

In thickets dense where silence reigns,
Unseen eyes watch, tethered by chains.
The rustling leaves speak tales of old,
Of secrets locked and terrors bold.

A whisper floats through the cool night air,
With every heartbeat, a hint of despair.
The shadows dance with muted grace,
Concealing truths in this dark embrace.

Muffled sounds of the forest roam,
Yet fear not, for it's their home.
Each silent watcher knows the way,
Through twisted paths where spirits play.

And when the moon casts a silver glow,
The unseen eyes begin to show.
A gleam of magic, a flicker of fright,
In the heart of the thickets, there dwells the night.

So tread with care, and hold your breath,
For in these woods, lies life and death.
An unseen gaze, a whispering sigh,
Beneath the boughs where the shadows lie.

Glistening Dew on Forgotten Trails

Upon the path where footsteps fade,
Glistening dew, a soft cascade.
Each droplet holds a world anew,
Reflecting dreams, the old and true.

In morning light, they shimmer bright,
A tapestry woven in sheer delight.
The trails remember the tales once spoken,
Of lost wanderers and hearts unbroken.

With every step, the echoes hum,
Of whispers passed, the long-lost drum.
Each dewy bead, a memory's trace,
Of journeys marked by time and space.

So follow the path where the dew will lead,
Through woodlands lush, a heart's quiet need.
With every drop, a story's told,
Of adventures bright, and treasures bold.

And when the sun begins to rise,
The trails will sparkle beneath the skies.
For in the dew, there lies a key,
To unlock the past, to set it free.

Beneath the Gloomy Canopy of Night

Beneath the gloom, the branches drape,
A shadowed world, a mystic shape.
The night conceals its keeper's grace,
In candle glow, we find our place.

With murmurs low, the world unfolds,
Beneath the night, a story told.
Each whispered breeze, a lover's sigh,
In darkness deep, the spirits fly.

The moon, a guardian shining bright,
Guides the lost through veils of night.
And in the stillness, hearts ignite,
A dance of shadows – a curious sight.

With every rustle in the leaves,
The magic weaves, the heart believes.
In twilight's cloak, we seek the stars,
Finding light in the darkest bars.

So take my hand, let's roam tonight,
Beneath the canopy, hearts alight.
For in the gloom, we find our spark,
And wander through the silent dark.

Journeying Through the Ensnaring Mist

In the hush of dawn's embrace,
Misty tendrils swiftly creep,
An adventure's heart laid bare,
Whispers where the shadows sleep.

Every step on cobblestone,
Brick by brick, a path unfolds,
With secrets hung in twilight air,
Fables spun of ancient gold.

Through wisps of fog, a figure sighs,
Tales untold in glimmers bright,
Their faces lost yet ever near,
Embracing both the day and night.

Past the gnarled and twisted trees,
Roots entwined in silence deep,
Onward through the silent pleas,
Where dreams and wanderlust leap.

In the depths of woven haze,
New horizons gently glow,
Guided by the starlit maze,
To the places spirits know.

The Call of Things Left Behind

In the attic, dust still sways,
A tenacious past remains,
Old toys whisper timeless tales,
Of laughter lost in twilight's veins.

Photographs in sepia hue,
Fleeting moments, smiles anew,
Echoes of the love once felt,
In each page, a heartbeats' cue.

Trinkets gathered through the years,
Dusty dreams and silent fears,
The shadows dance with fading light,
A tapestry of laughter, tears.

Yet in the corners, glimmers spark,
Memories flicker in the dark,
A call to cherish what has passed,
In every piece, a tiny mark.

As the days and seasons shape,
The lines of life, a fragile cape,
We hold the threads of yesteryears,
In our hearts they shall escape.

Murky Echoes of Arcane Songs

In the depths where shadows play,
Winds of magic softly sway,
Ancient echoes, cryptic tunes,
Calling forth the night from day.

Flickering flames in hollow caves,
Breathe the lore that time engraves,
Songs of wizards, lost and bold,
Whisper secrets of the braves.

Underneath the silver glow,
Footsteps wander to and fro,
Each refrain a thread of fate,
Entwined in the mystic flow.

In shadows thick the magics hum,
With every note, the ancients come,
Echoes of a world profound,
Where every silence speaks, and thrum.

As twilight spills its purple ink,
On hearts that throb and think,
Mysteries weaving through the air,
In murky depths, we dare to sink.

Stumbling Along the Greenway

On a path where wildflowers bloom,
A stumble leads to joyful tune,
Each step a dance with earthy glee,
In the green where breezes swoon.

Leaves rustle like a gentle cheer,
The sun's warm kiss, the sky so clear,
Amongst the trails we weave and wend,
The nature calls, forever near.

With laughter spilled like morning dew,
The whispers of the forest grew,
Birdsongs weave through branches high,
In a symphony, pure and true.

Beneath the arch of verdant skies,
Every glance reveals a prize,
A world where magic lightly strolls,
In every heart, pure wonder lies.

So stumble forth, embrace the way,
With open arms, let worries sway,
For in each twist and turn we find,
The beauty of a bright new day.

The Fog-Laden Forest's Fable

In the heart of the forest, mist creeps low,
Whispers of secrets the old trees know.
Branches like fingers, they beckon and sway,
Guiding lost souls who've wandered astray.

Beneath the thick shroud, shadows entwine,
Threads of enchantment in nature's design.
The air carries stories, both grim and bright,
A tapestry woven in the still of the night.

Mushrooms like lanterns glow soft and pale,
Leading the dreamers along winding trail.
Footsteps go silent, yet echoes remain,
In the fog-laden whispers of joy and pain.

A fox with bright eyes darts quick through the haze,
Chasing the flicker of twilight's last rays.
Deeper we wander, through thickets we weave,
Finding the fables that forests believe.

So linger a moment, let time hold its breath,
In the fog-laden woods, where dreams flirt with death.
In every sigh of the breeze, take heed,
For nature's own magic is what souls truly need.

Secrets Woven in the Evening Haze

As twilight drapes her velvet cloak,
The world holds secrets yet unspoke.
Stars wink softly, a celestial tease,
Whispers of lore ride the evening breeze.

Beneath the twilight, shadows play,
In the fading light, where night meets day.
Every flicker of light, a hidden tale,
In the tapestry woven where dreams set sail.

Moonlight weaves through the tangled trees,
Carrying murmurs on the gentle breeze.
A hush falls softly, the night takes its throne,
Embracing the quiet, a solitude known.

In the hush of the dusk, we find our place,
Amongst the secrets that time can't erase.
Each star a wish, each sigh a prayer,
In the evening haze, we breathe in the air.

So dance with the shadows, embrace the unknown,
In the evening's embrace, we are never alone.
For secrets lie hidden in the soft misty glow,
Waiting for dreamers who dare to let go.

Enigmas Wrapped in Vines of Darkness

In the depths of the night, where shadows entwine,
Whispers of enigmas in darkness align.
Vines wrap around thoughts like tendrils of fate,
Guarding the secrets that time won't debate.

Beneath the thick canopy, silence does breathe,
Hiding the puzzles that nature bequeath.
The world takes a pause, a moment so still,
As hearts seek the truth in the depths of their will.

Crickets are singing, a mystic refrain,
Notes floating softly, a sweet lingering pain.
Each rustle of leaves a riddle profound,
In the heart of the night, the answers are found.

Bats flit above in a shadowy dance,
Lost in the twilight, we take our chance.
The darkness embraces, a comforting shroud,
In its gentle hold, our dreams are allowed.

So linger in quiet where shadows doth play,
For enigmas wrapped in the night lead the way.
To learn of the mysteries with patience and grace,
In the vines of darkness, we find our true place.

The Dance of Shadows With the Stars

In the silent night, shadows stretch wide,
Dancing with stars in a velvety tide.
Whirls and twirls under a silver glow,
Each movement a story only night will bestow.

Footsteps of starlight, whispering low,
Guide us through places where stardust will flow.
Mysteries flutter like leaves in the air,
As shadows and stars engage in their fair.

With each gentle sway, the cosmos resounds,
Echoing laughter where joy knows no bounds.
An ethereal waltz, the heavens awake,
Stirring our spirits, our dreams they remake.

Embrace the soft chaos, let magic ignite,
In the dance of the shadows, take flight into night.
For every dark corner has secrets to tell,
In the company of stars, all is cast a spell.

So weave through the twilight, embrace the unknown,
In the dance of shadows, our hearts find a home.
For the rhythm of night hums a comforting tune,
Guiding our souls beneath the watchful moon.

Whispers of the Moonlit Thicket

Beneath the boughs where shadows play,
The moonlight spills in silver spray.
Creatures stir in the gentle night,
Each whisper wrapped in soft twilight.

With secrets spun in silken threads,
The thicket hums where magic spreads.
A soft breeze dances through the leaves,
While ancient spirits weave their weaves.

Stars peek through the velvet dark,
Casting dreams with a twinkling spark.
The world beyond fades into time,
In the thicket, all feels sublime.

Ethereal songs of the nightingale,
Bringing tales of the moon's pale trail.
In this cradle of whispered lore,
The heart finds peace forevermore.

So linger here where shadows blend,
In the moonlit hush, where wonders mend.
For every thicket holds its grace,
A hidden world, our secret place.

Shadows Cast by Ancient Trees

Among the giants, ancient and wise,
Tall stories linger under the skies.
With gnarled roots and branches wide,
They cradle tales of those who bide.

Each rustling leaf a voice from the past,
Echoing echoes that forever last.
In the dappled light where time stands still,
Life turns slowly upon the hill.

A tapestry woven of bark and lore,
Secret mysteries whisper and soar.
If you listen close, you'll hear their song,
A harmony sweet, where dreams belong.

Beneath the boughs, shadows dance and twist,
An enchanting world that can't be missed.
For in every shadow, a story grows,
Of love and loss that nature knows.

So walk the path where old trees sigh,
Beneath their watchful gaze, we lie.
For in their company, we find our way,
Guided by shadows, come what may.

The Sorceress's Forgotten Trails

In a realm where the wild river flows,
The sorceress wanders, her magic glows.
With flickering lanterns that twinkle bright,
She weaves her spells on the fabric of night.

Through woods where ivy proudly climbs,
She dances between the ancient rhymes.
With potions brewed from twilight's tears,
She whispers dreams that quell our fears.

Faint echoes linger in shadows near,
As she crafts enchantments, drawing us near.
The paths she walks are lost to time,
Yet every step holds a tale sublime.

Mysterious glades where secrets lie,
Breathing softly like a lonesome sigh.
With every flick of her graceful wrist,
She opens doors to the twilight mist.

So heed the trails where the magic flows,
For in her steps, the wonder grows.
With every turn in the hidden vale,
The sorceress waits along forgotten trails.

Veils of Mist in Enchanted Woods

In enchanted woods, the mist does weave,
A shroud of mystery that makes you believe.
Each tendril curls with a soft embrace,
Veiling the secrets of this magical space.

As dawn breaks gently through the haze,
The world awakens in a golden blaze.
With flickers of light and morning's breath,
Life twinkles softly in the hushed depth.

Hidden creatures stir in the quiet morn,
Whiskers twitch in the blush of dawn.
Every rustle, a tale yet told,
Of lands alive where wonders unfold.

Beneath the canopy, dreams take flight,
In the cool caress of the fading night.
Each ray that pierces the shroud of gray,
Unfolds tomorrow, a brand new day.

So roam these woods where magic stays,
In veils of mist, through sunlit rays.
For in each whisper and gentle spin,
A world of wonder awaits within.

Echoes of Secrets Beneath the Canopy

In the hush where whispers dwell,
Stories linger, soft as spells.
Moonlight dances, shadows gleam,
Secrets woven in a dream.

Branches sway with gentle grace,
Heartbeats quicken in this place.
Ancient roots and fleeting flight,
Nature guards her tales at night.

Each rustle speaks of lore untold,
In the dark, magic unfolds.
Fingers brush the cool, damp earth,
Beneath the stars, a hidden birth.

The breeze carries a calling sound,
Lost in wonder, all around.
The canopy, a guardian wide,
Holds the secrets deep inside.

Listen close, let silence reign,
In this world where shadows reign.
For every secret that we keep,
Beneath the canopy, they sleep.

Labyrinths of Twilight and Thorns

As daylight fades to twilight's grace,
A labyrinth unfolds its embrace.
Thorns like whispers, sharp yet fair,
Guide the dreamers unaware.

Moonlit paths twist, turn, and fold,
Stories of courage, brave and bold.
Each step echoes a heart's desire,
Leading souls through thorns and mire.

In the chill of the evening glow,
Mysteries wait, both high and low.
A flicker here, a shadow cast,
Where time weaves fables from the past.

Glimmers play in the evening mist,
Every turn, a chance not to miss.
In tangled roots, a fate awaits,
For the brave who dare to navigate.

Whispers lost in darkened halls,
Lure the night with beckoning calls.
In this maze of twilight and thorns,
A new adventure is reborn.

Ferns That Shiver in the Night

Beneath the stars, where shadows creep,
Ferns awaken from their sleep.
In the silence of the glade,
Magic stirs, unafraid.

Gentle rustles, soft and low,
Dance with secrets, ebb and flow.
Each frond unfurls, a tale begun,
In the embrace of night's soft sun.

Moonbeams kiss the verdant green,
Shimmering whispers, sight unseen.
With every breath, the forest sighs,
Ferns that shiver, hear their cries.

Nature hums its ancient song,
A melody where dreams belong.
In the stillness, voices rise,
Fleeting shadows in disguise.

As dawn approaches, soft and bright,
They fold beneath the coming light.
But in the dark, where secrets reign,
Ferns can shiver once again.

Beneath the Cowl of the Nightshade

Beneath the cowl where moonlight binds,
A world awakens, lost in minds.
Nightshade whispers, softly sings,
Of hidden truths and ancient things.

Among the roots, deep shadows lie,
With each breath, a gentle sigh.
Secrets wrapped in velvet dark,
Entwine with dreams, ignite a spark.

The stars above, they flicker low,
In the stillness, stories flow.
A dance of fate weaves through the leaves,
Entangled hopes, what one believes.

With every step, a journey calls,
Through twisted paths and shadowed walls.
In the nightshade's tender cloak,
Lies the promise of words unspoke.

Take a moment, pause, and breathe,
For in this space, our hearts believe.
Beneath the cowl of nightshade's grace,
Magic thrives in time and space.

A Glimmering Light in the Hollow

In the depths where shadows play,
A whisper calls from far away.
Through tangled roots and mossy stones,
A soft glow hums in gentle tones.

The nightingale sings a secret tune,
Beneath the watchful silver moon.
Each flicker bears a tale untold,
Of dreams and hopes in the dark enfold.

The hollow breathes with ancient sighs,
Where fireflies dance 'neath starlit skies.
A promise lingers, sweet and bright,
A glimmering light in the hollow's night.

As dawn begins to break anew,
The magic fades, yet lingers true.
With every step, a parting glance,
The echoes whisper, lost in trance.

In memory's keep, the tales reside,
Of glimmers caught on the ebbing tide.
For in the depths where shadows play,
A light resides, still shining, gay.

Spirits of the Underbrush

In the thicket where secrets roam,
Whispers stir like a home from loam.
Spirits twirl in a graceful dance,
Guided by fate, and not by chance.

Leaves rustle softly, a gentle sigh,
As shadows flutter and shadows fly.
Voices linger, familiar and near,
Calling to those who lend an ear.

Mossy blankets cover the ground,
Where unseen wonders can often be found.
A flicker of light, a breath of air,
The spirits linger, forever there.

Through bramble thick and orchids rare,
Magic weaves through the cool night air.
In the underbrush, hidden from sight,
Whispers and laughter dance in the light.

So tread with care, for they are awake,
These spirits dwell, each move they make.
In the wild where silence is gold,
Their ancient stories quietly unfold.

Enigmatic Turns in the Twilight

As twilight dims and shadows grow,
Paths twist and turn where few may go.
Mysteries beckon with subtle grace,
A fleeting glimpse of another place.

Gossamer threads weave the air so fine,
Guiding the lost through the arcane twine.
Each corner turned brings a gift anew,
Unraveled secrets just waiting for you.

Phantoms linger in the cool, still fog,
With voices soft as the night owl's clog.
In hushed tones, they share forgotten dreams,
Life's woven tale, bursting at the seams.

The stars awaken, a shimmering sea,
Illuminating all that cannot be.
As shadows dance and daylight wanes,
The twilight sighs, endless refrains.

So wander wise, let your heart be light,
For every turn holds a spark of delight.
In enigmatic shapes, let magic spill,
Turn with the twilight, feel the thrill.

The Green Veil of the Unfamiliar

Beyond the edge where wild things tread,
Lies a realm where few have fled.
A green veil shrouds the world obscure,
Holding mysteries both bright and pure.

With every leaf, a story weaves,
In the rustling whispers, the heart believes.
Lush canopies cradle the road unknown,
Where paths are grown and seeds are sown.

A flick of tail, a glint of eye,
Creatures brush past, like dreams that fly.
In each corner, enchantments coil,
Under the gaze of the stars' bright foil.

The air is thick with ancient lore,
Of heroes lost and battles bore.
In the woodland deep, the lost may find,
A way to heal the broken mind.

So venture forth through the verdant maze,
Let wonder cloak you in its gentle blaze.
For in the heart of the wild's embrace,
Lies the green veil of the unfamiliar place.

Lessons in the Weaving Mist

In whispers soft, the mist does weave,
Secrets old, for those who believe.
A tapestry of dreams unfolds,
In every thread, a story told.

With every dawn, the fog reveals,
The magic lurking, the heart feels.
Through shadows deep, and glimmers bright,
We learn to dance in pure delight.

The lessons learned in twilight's grace,
Guide us gently, a warm embrace.
In weaving paths where spirits roam,
We find ourselves, we find our home.

A tapestry of fate is spun,
In mists where dreams and daylight run.
Through veils of fog, our spirits soar,
With lessons learned, we seek for more.

So tread with care, dear wanderer bold,
In whispers sweet, let your heart be sold.
For in the mist, the truth lies bare,
A lesson cloaked in evening air.

Forest Songs of the Bewitched

In ancient woods where echoes play,
The trees sing songs of a hidden day.
With leaves that shimmer in twilight's glow,
They tell of wonders that none may know.

Bewitched by sprites and playful sprites,
The forest hums with ethereal lights.
A melody carried on gentle breeze,
In every rustle, a dance of leaves.

Each step we take on mossy ground,
Resonates with the magic found.
In whispers soft, the night unveils,
The secrets held in nature's trails.

The owls converse in wise refrain,
While shadows play a lover's game.
Each chorus wraps us, warm and tight,
In forest songs that weave the night.

So listen close, dear heart of stone,
The woods will sing, you're not alone.
In every note, a spell is cast,
In haunted woods, you'll dance at last.

Enchantment's Grip on Charmed Trails

On trails where sunlight softly gleams,
Enchantment whispers in the dreams.
Each step we take, a spell reborn,
In nature's cradle, our souls are worn.

With every twist, the path unfolds,
A story hidden, a truth it holds.
The air is thick with magic's art,
As shadows waltz and pull the heart.

In ink and moss, the secrets dwell,
A tale of love and fleeting spell.
With every breath, we taste the lore,
Of charm that weaves through every door.

The winding road may lead to fate,
With laughter sweet, and whispers great.
For in this dance, we find our part,
In enchantment's grip, we feel the heart.

So wander forth, through verdant glades,
Let magic flourish in the shades.
Embrace the trails where wonders bloom,
In charmed embrace, dispelling gloom.

The Stolen Steps of the Wanderer

In quiet dusk, the wanderer walks,
On hidden paths where shadow talks.
With stolen steps, he glides along,
A fleeting note in the world's song.

Through winding lanes with whispered tales,
A spirit wanders where hope prevails.
Each footprint marks a tale untold,
In twilight's grasp, the night unfolds.

Yet in the stillness, secrets bloom,
The wanderer seeks a brighter room.
In every corner, a magic spark,
Guides the lost within the dark.

His heart a compass, it points the way,
To dreams unbound, where shadows sway.
Each stolen step, a dance divine,
With every heartbeat, stars align.

So take your journey, embrace the night,
For in these steps, you'll find your light.
The wanderer knows, with every breath,
There's beauty found in life and death.

Starlit Journeys through the Boughs

Underneath the twinkling skies,
Adventurers gather, laughter flies.
Through whispering leaves and fluttering dreams,
Magic sparkles in moonlit beams.

With wishes tucked in pockets tight,
They wander far into the night.
Verdant paths where shadows play,
Guided by the stars' ballet.

Each branch a stories' gentle grin,
Inviting secrets from within.
The air is thick with scents of pine,
A map uncharted but divine.

Beneath the gaze of ancient trees,
Time dances like the evening breeze.
They sing of journeys yet to start,
Carved in every wanderer's heart.

So step into the wild embrace,
Where adventure waits in every space.
With every step beneath the lights,
The world awakens to new heights.

The Sorceress's Secret Passage

A hidden door with ivy clad,
Leads to whispers good and bad.
Beneath the stone, a spell that's cast,
Echoes from a long-lost past.

Candles flicker on the wall,
Illuminating shadows tall.
Potions bubble with secrets spun,
Where magic sleeps 'til day is done.

In every nook, an ancient tome,
Of wizards, witches, and a home.
Brightly colored jars aligned,
A treasure trove for curious minds.

Along this path where few have tread,
Mysteries rise like morning thread.
For those with courage, hearts so pure,
The sorceress will guide them sure.

So venture forth with steady hand,
Through hidden realms, you'll understand.
Each step a journey, every clue,
Revealing worlds both old and new.

Forgotten Ways in the Twilight Forest

In the forest where shadows blend,
Whispers of the lost descend.
Forgotten trails woven in mist,
Invite the brave to twist and twist.

Through tangled roots and silken leaves,
Old enchantments cling like thieves.
A tapestry of dusk and dreams,
Sewing light with fading gleams.

Each pathway tells a tale once told,
Of ancient warriors, brave and bold.
The moonlight weaves a silver path,
Calling forth the morning's wrath.

With every step, the magic hums,
Echoes of enchanted drums.
Among the trees, a spirit calls,
A dancing shadow that enthralls.

So wander deep, let heart ignite,
In twilight's arms, find your light.
For in the whispers, brave and true,
Lies a journey meant for you.

Gnarled Roots and Wandering Souls

In the grove where old trees sigh,
Gnarled roots spread beneath the sky.
With stories woven in their bark,
They cradle dreams both bright and dark.

Wandering souls pause on their way,
To rest where shadows softly play.
The branches stretch like arms in prayer,
As secrets drift upon the air.

Each knot and twist, a tale to tell,
Of love, of loss, where hearts once fell.
The earth holds whispers of the past,
Eternity in moments cast.

With every breeze that lingers near,
The spirits of the forest cheer.
In harmony, they dance and sway,
Embracing night, embracing day.

So seek this place of ancient lore,
Where roots entwine and spirits soar.
For in this grove, with every glance,
You'll find the world still holds its chance.

Where the Moonlight Fears to Tread

In shadows deep where whispers dwell,
The air is thick with stories to tell.
A silver glow, it quivers and fades,
As secrets hide in moonlit glades.

Beneath the trees where owls take flight,
The world holds breaths, the stars shine bright.
Each footprint lost in the night's embrace,
Leaves a trace of a hidden place.

A glimmer sparks in the velvet gloom,
Where time stands still, and dreams must bloom.
A dance of shadows, a fleeting glance,
Where wishes linger and souls might dance.

For in this realm where light won't stray,
Mysteries call and hearts won't sway.
So venture forth, but heed the dread,
For not all paths where moonlight led.

Unravel tales and heed them true,
The twilight songs that softly flew.
For in this night, where silence reigns,
The heart of magic forever remains.

The Prayer of the Twisted Roots

Beneath the boughs of ancient trees,
Where the wind carries forgotten pleas.
Twisted roots in the earth unwind,
A prayer for those lost to time.

Whispers echo in the stillness found,
In shadows deep, where fate is bound.
Each knot and twist tells tales of woe,
A dance with history, both fast and slow.

The forest breathes a sleepful sigh,
A cradle for dreams that flit and fly.
Each leaf that falls leaves memories spun,
In this sacred space, we are all one.

So offer your heart to the secrets kept,
Embrace the depths where shadows wept.
For every root that grips the stone,
Holds stories of life, experiences sown.

A tapestry woven in earth and sky,
Marks the passage of those who try.
Where roots intertwine, a bond so true,
Is the prayer of the twisted, made anew.

A Journey Through Shrouded Realms

Through veils of fog, the path leads on,
To realms where light and shadow blend, drawn.
A journey sought with wonder and fear,
Each step reveals what's far and near.

The air is thick with magic's song,
Where worlds of old and new belong.
A bridge of stars, it flickers bright,
Guides the way through the endless night.

With whispered hopes beneath my breath,
I walk the line 'twixt life and death.
Creatures watch with knowing eyes,
In their wisdom, the truth lies.

Each turn I take, the mystery deepens,
Where laughter echoes, and silence steepens.
A riddle's heart beats within the night,
As shadows dance, both bold and light.

So onward still, I tread the path,
Unraveling tales, embracing the wrath.
For in this realm where dreams unfurl,
Life and magic's tales gently twirl.

Flickering Lanterns in Enchanted Murk

In the murk where secrets dwell,
Flickering lanterns cast their spell.
A golden glow through shadows deep,
Awakens dreams from restless sleep.

Each lantern sways in the midnight breeze,
Guide my steps with whispered pleas.
In the tangled woods, where echoes play,
The night reveals the somber day.

With every flicker, a vision born,
Of history, pain, and hearts still worn.
Each flame a beacon, each shadow a shade,
A dance of light in the twilight made.

Through tangled paths and stories sown,
I wander deep, yet not alone.
For lanterns bright will light the way,
In enchanted murk, come what may.

So let your heart be brave and true,
In every flicker, find what's new.
For in this realm where night reveals,
The magic speaks, and love it heals.

Paths of Shadow and Silhouette

In twilight's grip, the shadows play,
Flickering forms that drift away.
Beneath the moon's soft silken glow,
Pathways twist where whispers go.

A silhouette against the night,
A haunting presence, barely sight.
Footsteps echo on cobblestone,
In the silence, one stands alone.

Branches weave like darkened dreams,
Echoing soft, forgotten themes.
Mist enshrouds the winding trail,
Of secrets where the shadows sail.

With every turn, a choice is made,
In shadows deep, no light will fade.
Yet courage stirs in heart's deep core,
For in the dark, there's much in store.

Through paths of shadow, guiding light,
Awakens strength in endless night.
For even dark holds stories bright,
When souls unite in shared delight.

The Flicker of Forgotten Light

In corners dim, a warm glow fades,
Once vibrant sparks in twilight parades.
Flickers dance on worn-out walls,
Remnants of laughter, distant calls.

A lantern's flame, now dim and slight,
Holds whispers of a long-lost night.
Shadows throw their playful spells,
While silence weaves its whispered wells.

What dreams have wandered through this space?
What joy once lit the shadowed place?
Each flicker holds a tale untold,
Of hearts once brave, and spirits bold.

Yet hope remains in every spark,
A chance to light the deepest dark.
With trembling hands, the light ignites,
Reviving joy on those starless nights.

For in the flicker lies the flame,
A beacon bright, it calls your name.
Embrace the glow, rekindle flight,
In memories' dance, find pure delight.

Chasing Dreams in the Murky Depths

Beneath the surface, dreams reside,
Tangled in currents, nowhere to hide.
Through murky waters, visions swirl,
In shadowed hush, ambitions twirl.

Each ripple whispers tales of plight,
Of hopes once gleaming, now out of sight.
Yet still we chase those fleeting beams,
With hearts ablaze, igniting dreams.

In the depths where darkness clings,
A glimmer glows, the thrill it brings.
Through eerie depths, brave souls will dive,
In search of light where wishes strive.

Underwater worlds, alive with grace,
Emerald hues in a somber place.
Yet courage knows no bounds in night,
In murky depths, we seek the light.

So chase those dreams, let spirits soar,
In the murk, we'll find much more.
For every shadow hides a quest,
To turn the depths into our nest.

Shadowed Breezes in the Hollowed Woods

In hollowed woods where secrets sigh,
The shadowed breezes whisper by.
Leaves rustle soft, a gentle tune,
Beneath the watchful, silver moon.

Twisting paths where shadows blend,
Echoes call, and branches bend.
Mossy carpets cradle feet,
In hidden realms where spirits meet.

Every breeze tells tales of old,
Of wanderers brave and hearts so bold.
In every gust, a story stirs,
Of dreams that drift like whispered furs.

As twilight deepens, shadows stretch,
In nature's arms, a soul can etch.
Through hollowed woods, we find our way,
With shadowed breezes leading stray.

So wander on where magic flows,
In every dark, a light still glows.
In shadowed woods, let spirits play,
And guide your heart to brighter days.

Veils of Mist and Memory

In the glade where shadows weave,
A whisper beckons, hard to believe.
Glimmers of past in a silvery sigh,
Traveling moments that flutter and fly.

Veils of mist dance softly so,
Guiding the heart where lost souls go.
Echoes of laughter bathed in the air,
Serenading dreams with a tender care.

Through emerald graces, secrets unfold,
Stories of ages in silence told.
Ripples of time flow gently and slow,
Carving new paths where the wildflowers grow.

Yet shadows linger, whispering fears,
As daylight fades and night draws near.
Memories shimmer, bittersweet light,
In the veils of mist that cloak the night.

When dawn emerges, the magic will sway,
Carrying whispers from yesterday.
The heart stays tethered, forever entwined,
In the mists of memory, solace you'll find.

Moonlit Footsteps in the Fog

Beneath the glow of a silvered moon,
Footsteps echo, a haunting tune.
Shrouded in fog where the shadows dance,
Whispers beckon with a strange romance.

Ghostly figures drift in the gloom,
Serenading the night with soft perfume.
Each step taken leads to a spark,
Illuminating dreams hidden in the dark.

Chasing the stars, they weave and sway,
Guiding lost wanderers who've lost their way.
Crickets serenade, a gentle refrain,
In the moonlit canvas, connection remains.

Yet beware the chill of the midnight breeze,
For darkness can linger, never to tease.
With every heartbeat, the magic unfolds,
In moonlit footsteps, a tale retold.

As the night wanes and the dawn appears,
Echoes of fog dissolve like fears.
Footprints vanish with the rising sun,
Leaving behind all that was done.

Echoes of the Hidden Glen

In a glen hidden from worldly strife,
Nature whispers secrets, breathing life.
A symphony plays between trees so tall,
As echoes of laughter, the fairies call.

Sunlight dapples through the emerald leaves,
Casting its magic as the heart believes.
Flowers burst forth in jubilant cheer,
Swaying with grace, inviting us near.

Yet shadows linger on the forest floor,
Guarding the tales of the days of yore.
Ancient oaks stand, their stories profound,
In the hidden glen where wisdom is found.

The song of the brook flows gently and clear,
As echoes of memories draw ever near.
Each ripple a whisper of dreams long past,
In the glen of enchantment, where time is cast.

As twilight descends with a tender sigh,
Stars wink above in the velvet sky.
In the hidden glen where magic grows,
The echoes remain, as the night bestows.

Lurking in the Gloomy Shade

In the corners where shadows creep,
Murmurs of secrets begin to seep.
Figures linger in the twilight's embrace,
Guarding the stories, a hidden place.

Lurking softly in gloomy shade,
Whispers of past, a masquerade.
Branches entwine like fingers in prayer,
Draped in mystery, a tale to share.

Beneath the boughs where silence reigns,
Echoes of longing in soft refrains.
The heart beats louder with each rustling leaf,
As shadows gather, cloaked in belief.

Yet in that darkness, there's beauty bright,
A flicker of hope, a glimpse of light.
In the gloom, there's magic to find,
Hidden in whispers, softly designed.

When dawn appears and shadows disperse,
The stories emerge, both blessed and cursed.
From lurking depths where the silence played,
Awakening dreams in the gloomy shade.

Riddles Hidden Beneath Leafy Canopies

In the embrace of ancient trees,
Where whispers twist and dance with ease,
Secrets ripple through the leaves,
And into curious minds it weaves.

Footsteps softly trace the ground,
Mysteries in silence found,
A riddle waits in shadows' veil,
Tales of magic and of frail.

Beneath the boughs, the stories weave,
Of daring hearts that dare believe,
Unlocking doors from deep within,
To where the wild and wise begin.

With every flutter, every sigh,
The forest breathes, it does not lie,
Its riddles sung in rustled sound,
An ancient language all around.

So wander forth with open mind,
Beneath the leafy arms, you'll find,
In every shadow, each soft glare,
A riddle waits for those who dare.

The Faint Glow of the Lurking Sage

Amidst the ruins, shadowed, deep,
A sage resides, his wisdom keep,
With eyes like twilight, ever wise,
His thoughts a dance beneath the skies.

A faint glow glimmers through the night,
Guiding lost souls with gentle light,
He murmurs secrets, soft and low,
Of journeys taken long ago.

In hidden places, time stands still,
Where nature bends to magic's will,
The sage knows paths that few have trod,
And speaks in riddles, a gift from God.

So linger close, and heed his call,
In whispered tones, he'll tell you all,
Of ancient dreams and futures bright,
In every shadow, a spark of light.

The lurking sage, a silent guide,
With wisdom vast, he won't divide,
In his embrace, you'll find your way,
Through tangled thoughts to break of day.

Secrets of the Starless Woods

In woods where starlight dares not tread,
The whispers of the lost are spread,
A shroud of dreams in shadows spun,
Where shadows play and time's undone.

Beneath the boughs, old stories writ,
Of every wanderer who dared to sit,
In silence deep, a secret sigh,
Awaiting hearts that wander by.

The trees embrace the twilight gloom,
A dance of echoes through the bloom,
They guard the past, the hopes, the fears,
And every laugh that turned to tears.

With every step, a tale unfolds,
In places dark, where night enfolds,
The starless woods, a world apart,
With secrets held in nature's heart.

So tread with care, and eyes wide bright,
For hidden truths will come to light,
In whispers soft, the woods will sing,
Of all the magic that they bring.

A Dance Among Weeping Willows

Beneath the boughs of willow trees,
Where shadows sway in gentle breeze,
A dance begins, both soft and slow,
In moonlit glade where dreamers go.

The branches weep with grace and sigh,
As stars above begin to fly,
With every twirl, a story spun,
Of hopes and loves beneath the sun.

In twilight's glow, the dancers gleam,
Their laughter ripples like a stream,
With hearts entwined, they lose their cares,
In every step, a world that shares.

The willows sway, their whispers light,
In gentle folds through softest night,
Where souls unite in twirls and spins,
A dance of wonder that begins.

So join the dance, let spirits soar,
Among the willows, we'll explore,
In every laugh, a memory stays,
In the weeping trees, a song always.

9 781805 630227